April Mae's
WORST
of
hopeless
hints

April Mae's
WORST
of
hopeless
hints

with
Simon Dublin

PRICE/STERN/SLOAN
Publishers, Inc., Los Angeles
1983

ISBN: 0-8431-0722-7

DEDICATION

This book
is dedicated to
all of those who are
usually at a loss,
helpless in the great majority of situations,
completely incompetent around the house,
usually unable to cope,
and a nervous wreck in minor disasters.

CONTENTS

Every single **APRIL MAE BRAND**® item from our fine family of products is guaranteed to have been personally thought up by me at sometime or other, and is certain to be 1000 percent effective if used in a conscientiously applied program of oral hygiene and regular professional care.

(NOTE: **APRIL MAE BRAND**® products can be mailed to you, upon your request, in a plain brown paper wrapper. See page 94.)

FOREWORD

So, you've just spilled red wine all over your best tablecloth and your hubby says it doesn't go with the fish stains? Then this is the book for you.

April Mae—the author of this book—is known personally to me. I have been her neighbor for 37 years.

I can say honestly that I have always admired and respected April Mae.

Of course, I've never liked her very much. Frankly, I have grown sick and tired of fending off her attempts to crash my dinner parties, empty my wine cellar, and hawk the home-made elixirs, solvents and contraptions made by her lunatic of a husband. In fact, I have been unable to get the deep spots made by **April Mae Brand®️ Nail Polish Helper** off my make-up table now for 29 years.

Nevertheless I *have* admired April Mae, because she works harder at her incompetence and helplessness than anyone I have *ever* known.

I *respect* April Mae, too, for the persistence she has shown through the years in rounding up an impressive collection of the wrong advice—in a multitude of situations, from literally hundreds of incompetent friends, relatives and neighbors.

April Mae has organized the most outstanding of her helpless hints into convenient categories for ready reference.

In this way, you can have rapid access to her wrong advice.

In fact, against my better judgement, (perhaps because we are neighbors), I have actually followed April Mae's advice, and I can testify to the fact that she has been wrong consistently.

Incidentally, I tried the **Chief Executive Panty Hose**® on page 33, and it did more than just run for President. It also ran for *me*.

Have I said that I do not like April Mae's husband? Any man who mows the lawn with a crumb-scraper to save gasoline cannot have all of his porch lights on. In my respectful opinion.

Yours very sincerely,

Calamity Merriweather

INTRODUCTION

I am just fit to be tied—and sick and tired of talking to young women who say they're just hopeless around the house!

It seems to me there just isn't enough optimism and stick-to-it-iveness in this glass-is-half-empty society!

Oh, you've left the beer in the freezer and it blew up? Let me tell you, I once left my husband in the freezer and I can tell you *he* blew up.

You say the man of the house is leaving because you're such a bad housekeeper? Well, let him run *off* with a housekeeper. They both deserve each other, if you ask me.

My dears, you've got to adopt a positive attitude: You can *solve* your household problems the April Mae way! How? Like this:

● Are you tired of seeing lint on dark rugs? Just shampoo them with Head and Shoulders!

● Do you find your hubby's romantic technique putting you to sleep? Then just try setting the snooze alarm on the bedroom clock radio!

● Do you have a tough time drying your nails rapidly? Well, just lash yourself to the lawn sprinkler and go for a spin!

My dears, it's look-'em-straight-in-the-eyes time!!! Take heart! You can do ANYTHING if you'll (1) Just read every word of this book, and (2) Send away for a few of my **APRIL MAE BRAND**® products.

Have a Nice Day,

April Mae

11

HINTS FOR CHILDREN

The thing that I, April Mae, cannot understand about parents nowadays is: Why do they have so many problems with their kids?

So many bright, attractive young parents tell me all about their problems after they introduce themselves to me on my many popular personal appearance tours (and if you're interested, dears, just write April Mae's manager, my husband, at the address given at the end of the book!).

To return to the subject at hand, what Mom needs is some good, old-fashioned advice! You'll never go wrong if you keep in mind April Mae's Four Children's Pointers:

1. No parent has ever failed with peanut butter.

2. When Benjamin Spock lets you down, perhaps Jack Daniel's can be of assistance.

3. Disregard all the nasty things that you've heard people say about children, like that time when W.C. Fields said about changing diapers, "I'd rather be in Philadelphia." April Mae has made many public appearances in Philadelphia (for very reasonable speakers' fees) and I just think it's a fine town.

4. If you're at a loss about how to handle upstart kids, remember this: You'll never go wrong if you'll treat 'em as firmly as you handle the biggest kid in the house, your hubby.

Gum remedy
- The children's bubble gum may be removed from mommy's hair in a jiffy by putting her in the refrigerator and then scraping off the gum when it hardens.

Save those old baby-food jars
- You'll find that used baby-food jars are especially good for saving and keeping around the kitchen and not being used for very much of anything at all.

Emergency teddy bear
- In a pinch, if you've misplaced a tot's stuffed animal, you'll find it easy to substitute a sleeping husband for a child's missing teddy bear.

String along with mom
- Simply string child's gloves to jacket, child's jacket to child, child to mother, and mother to soft mattress.

Scraped knees
- Scraped knees will never be a problem if you'll raise your child exclusively on rubber mats.

Feeding a "spitter," using the Lloyd Bridges method.

Here's food in your eye

- Tired of that tot who's a "spitter," sitting in the high chair and getting baby food all over the kitchen? Mom'll stay dry simply by wearing wet suit, face mask and flippers, while dad may find that a waterproof camera housing is best for those photo sessions in the kitchen.

Pampered in an emergency

- In conditions of extreme cold, an excellent sleeping bag can be constructed by tying 450 Pampers together with dental floss. The resultant covering has been shown to protect sleeping mothers, fathers and children down to temperatures of minus 30 degrees.

- Scientists at the Woods Hole Oceanographic Institution have demonstrated to April Mae that, using 4,322 Pampers, masking tape and a bicycle pump, shipwrecked survivors can construct a small raft which can accomodate 12 parents, 22 children and their pets, keeping them afloat for as long as four months.

- For an unusual conversation piece, bronze baby's first Pamper and put it on the mantelpiece!

- Pampers can be stored in the attic to reduce home heating bills substantially during the winter!

Portable mattress

- Remember: On those overnight trips, a tired, inebriated husband always makes an excellent and reliable mattress for a sleeping child.

The one sleeping bag you can't order from L. L. Bean.

Child's play
● Don't throw away those burnt marshmallows and hot dogs from the family picnic . . . they make nifty mobiles for baby's crib.

17

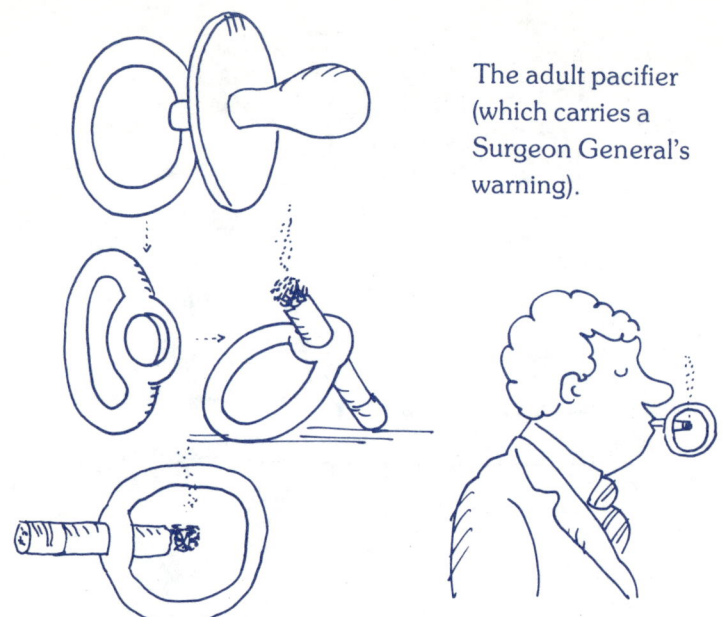

The adult pacifier
(which carries a
Surgeon General's
warning).

Pacification program

- Those old, used pacifiers must be carefully saved if they are to be made into center-pieces, pierced earrings or surprisingly efficient drywall insulation material. In a pinch, a pacifier may be affixed to a car radio antenna to signal that the driver is in distress.

- Old pacifiers should be saved and collected, since they are very useful for throwing at old ladies in the park who say you're holding the baby wrong.

A book at the seat of knowledge
- In a pinch, the paperback edition of Dr. Spock's "Baby and Child Care" makes an excellent and highly absorbent diaper if the book is split into sections and used to line baby's rubber pants.

Keeping your kids creased
- After youngsters have put on their best duds, lightly mist clothes with hair spray! Those kids will look crisp and pressed for hours!

To be or knot to be
- Wise moms know: It is very hard to teach your youngster how to tie her shoes, but it's a cinch to teach her to run to daddy for help tying!

A tux for the toddler
- Afraid your mother-in-law will think you're too casual a mom? For a more formal look, on her next visit polish baby's little pajama feet with black shoe polish.

Putting on the dog
- An April Mae caution: Remember, no matter how energetic your toddler is, in 17 states it is a criminal offense to put that little explorer on a leash!

Don't let bad weather drive you nuts

● Stuck with nothing to do with those kids on a rainy morning? Try making peanut butter sculptures of Big Macs and fries! Then eat 'em up for lunch!

Replacing those lost rubbers

● In a pinch, color up some Baggies with black Magic Marker and slip them over your kid's shoes.

Table paste for a summer white buck look

● Has your bouncing baby outgrown shoes again? Dab black or brown shoe polish all over your toddler's feet for a money-saving shoe substitute.

LAUNDRY HINTS

I will never *ever* forget the first time I folded laundry in the nude! I would not ordinarily be revealing this remarkable secret of successful modern laundry management to you. However, since you have paid your money (which is now on deposit in April Mae's personal account here in the First County Bank) I will tell you that your friend April Mae does not mean to say by this that she *ever* does anything *naughty* while folding the laundry. It is true that my hubby, who is always puttering around the basement making many of the **April Mae Brand®** line of fine products in his workshop, has seen me folding laundry on occasion. In fact, he has frequently been *inspired* by the very sight of April Mae folding the laundry, dressed just as Nature made her.

To sum up, then: When April Mae does this humble little work-a-day chore without a stitch of clothing on, it makes her feel free, spontaneous, healthy, and at one with the naturalness of the laundry environment. And it gets hubby helping in the laundry room just as quick as you can say Sally Rand!

All about lint

- Remember that lint is actually a very delicate animal that mates and reproduces rapidly in automatic clothes dryers and sometimes in your pockets as well.

- Lint may be harvested from the lint trap and used as an inexpensive replacement for goose down filler!

Sticky drawers

- Prevent this problem by laundering the items more carefully.

Cold pants for comfort

- Damp laundry kept in the refrigerator for ironing can also be frozen for wearing during muggy summer days.

Perky pre-soak

- For a fun-filled pre-soak, simply drape the soiled laundry over your body and shower with a friend.

Spilled wine, a rug, and thou

- Those rug-soaking spills of wine, beer, Scotch and gin can be sopped up quickly and enjoyably with the tongue.

HINTS FOR CLOTHES

Although I have long been known to my many friends, neighbors and fans as one of the country's most know-ledgeable experts in the fast-growing field of modern clothing management and maintenance, I find that many young homemakers ask me just one question, and one question only:

"April Mae," they wonder, "Why should I buy your **April Mae Brand® Designer Jeans?**"

Can you guess what I tell them? Well, I smile. I place a motherly hand on their shoulder, and I tell them this:

"You should buy **April Mae Brand® Designer Jeans** because ONLY my jeans have been specially tailored by April Mae herself to fit both you AND your hubby!"

On the run
- Even your newest pantyhose will run quickly and permanently if you'll simply look at it the wrong way, think about it unkindly, or turn your back on it for a minute.

The sticky zipper caper
- Even the stickiest zipper is a good bet to jam completely if you'll just panic and use the pliers.

Delicate white things
- April Mae's folks always remember that the fundamental purpose of white garments is to be stained.

- It's a cinch to remove those soiled blotches from white garments partially, so that they'll always remind you of your frustration at not being able to clean them totally.

- April Mae's handy rule about white things: You can be confident that any white shirt, pants, dress, scarf, sweater or jacket will attract a stain within about seven minutes of wearing.

Those odd socks

- Don't know what to do with those pairs of mismatched socks? Try wearing them out of the house for the entertainment of friends, neighbors, co-workers, and the boss.

Best jeans

- Washing that favorite pair of designer jeans enough to make it fit perfectly will make it possible to rip them apart with the slightest wrong motion.

Designer gold brings slivered threads.

No sweat about sweaters

- Just about any sweater is sure to lose its shape if stored flat, folded, unfolded or hung.

- April Mae's handy rule: The more handsome and bulky the knit, the more intolerably scratchy the sweater.

A straight razor will smooth out even a Scandinavian ski sweater.

Some wrinkles on wrinkles

- That newly pressed skirt or pants can be wrinkled with but a single climb behind the steering wheel of your automobile.

- A recent pressing of any garment is a truly excellent forecaster of torrential rain.

Shrinkable garments and a leaky umbrella will end any drought.

The pattern patterns

- The helpful illustration on the pattern envelope is certain to look completely unlike the finished dress.

- Use an electric scissors and it's a cinch to cut not only that dress pattern but the tablecloth as well.

- Did you know? Your old undies may be saved, bundled and sold for a high price to the American Grand Order of Odd Fellows, where they will be cherished.

A peach of an idea

- Need to replace the expensive goose fluff leaking out of your down coat? You'll save money on prime goose down if you'll just shave your peaches and use the fuzz!

And ask yourself . . .

**"Isn't it time to try
APRIL MAE BRAND®
CHIEF EXECUTIVE PANTY HOSE?"**

Manufactured exclusively by my hubby—who is past president of the Grand Sacred Order of Friendly Traffic Rotaries of America—we are proud to offer *April Mae Brand® Chief Executive Panty Hose:* It's guaranteed to run only for President!

See page 94 to learn how to order.

HINTS FOR FLOORS

My friends, more than one back fence friendship has been dashed to smithereens when a foolhardy homemaker lets the other folks on the block think that she's too ambitious in the shiny-floor department.

Can't you see your neighbor's husband coming in one day and saying, "Hi, Honey, I'm home, and how come you don't have floors as clean as Jane's?"

Stop your worrying. *You* can have clean floors *and* the esteem of your neighbors as well!

How is this possible? I would like to take the liberty here of doing a "plug" for **April Mae Brand® Waxy Yellow Buildup.**

This product will enable you to have your floors *and* your neighbors, too. Go ahead, *keep* floors shiny, and maintain a tidy house that will make your hubby proud.

But when the neighbors are due for a sudden visit, a quick application of **April Mae Brand® Waxy Yellow Buildup** will leave your floors dull and faded-looking. It'll put those visitors right at ease!

Remember, **April Mae Brand® Waxy Yellow Buildup** is harvested at considerable effort from April Mae's own kitchen and rec room floors.

Stubborn heel marks
- Heel marks will never be much of a problem on floors that are kept truly dirty.

For dust balls
- Although dustballs make quite excellent collectibles, they'll never attain very large sizes if you sweep, clean and vacuum too ambitiously.

Ingenuity can lead you to new ways to "scale" old wax off linoleum.

Rockin'-chair scratches
- That old rocking chair can't mark your floors if they're protected by a good, thick coating of waxy yellow buildup.

When all else fails
- In a pinch, an active and unsteady toddler in pajamas can frequently be used as an excellent floor polisher.

Absolutely floored
- A strong mixture of ammonia and water, sitting in a pail on the kitchen floor, can make an entire kitchen uninhabitable. In time, it can take care of a medium-sized house.

Carpet sweepings
- Although your old carpet sweeper is less effective than a modern vacuum cleaner, it can certainly spill its entire messy contents on your rug much more quickly and easily.

Fading floors
- As little as half an hour's exposure to bright sunlight each day is an excellent, no-work way of fading those vinyl floor coverings.

Vacuum-cleaner bag hint

- As many as 20 to 30 square yards of clean carpet can be completely dirtied by an exploding vacuum cleaner bag if you'll forget to replace it for long enough.

The knees have it

- Want a no-work way to dust the garage floor? Encourage the kids to have all their marbles tournaments there.

Straighten that rug

- Do your rugs curl up at the edges? Try shampooing them with laundry starch!

Uncornered

- Painted yourself into a corner while shellacking the rec-room floor? (1) Remove shoes and socks, (2) shellac your feet, and (3) walk right on out of there!

Snug as a bug

- A rug-gripper: Just swathe that crawling baby in a Velcro diaper and he'll always stay put on the living room rug!

And have you tried . . .

APRIL MAE BRAND® LIQUID MOP!

A remarkable liquid that may be used on every surface from kitchen floors to patio tiles, this product is made exclusively in April Mae's hubby's basement according to his own secret formula.

April Mae Brand® Liquid Mop is an extraordinary liquid: it is clear, wet, nontoxic, may be mixed with detergent or cleansers, may be drunk safely to quench the thirst, and bears an incredible resemblance to tap water from April Mae's laundry sink!

Please see page 94 to learn how to order.

AUTO HINTS

In many years of experience with every kind of automobile in every conceivable state of disrepair and disfunction, April Mae has always followed one cardinal rule.

Pretend:
(1) You know absolutely nothing about automobiles,

(2) You don't *care* about automobiles,

(3) You couldn't even open the dashboard if you had a can opener,

(4) You never knew that tires had to be changed, and

(5) By the way, what's a tire?

This seemingly simple advice has given April Mae a lifetime of freedom from worry about any sort of automobile problem whatsoever. It has made my hubby feel happy and useful. It has helped a huge population of garage mechanics to feel important, superior and effective.

April Mae's attitude is very simple: Why let anyone else guess just *how much* you know about automobiles? So April Mae advises you to study the fine advice that follows:

Car-battery care
- An automobile battery is guaranteed not to turn over if you'll only leave it dry enough for long enough.

Automobile rug-a-marole
- With proper care (irrigation in the form of perspiration and the use of fertilizers) the dirt in the rugs and seat covers of the average family's automobile will yield a rich harvest of green vegetables, legumes and hardy perennials.

Substitute auto antennas
- Remember: An old wire coat hanger, if used to replace a broken car radio antenna, will be useless in holding a pair of pants.

Glove-compartment component
- An ordinary ball-point pen or a pencil, if stored in the glove compartment of the average-sized family automobile, will never ever be found again.

After using the flame
technique, be certain
to put glove back on
before opening door.

Those frozen locks
● Just hold the flame from a match or cigarette
lighter to the keyhole of a frozen automobile
lock and you'll surely be able to open the door
and bubble your body paint. See "Opening
Frozen Bagels."

Car won't start?
● Leave the automobile unlocked on an isolated
street with the key in the ignition—soon that
engine will spring to life!

Outdoor sculpture
● Old snow tires may be used as distinctive outdoor collectibles, as long as you have understanding neighbors.

An inexpensive snow tire may be fashioned out of old ski boots.

Ashes to ashes
- The ashtray in the family car will never have to be cleaned for the entire life span of the vehicle if it is simply ignored.

Car theft no more
- Car theft will never ever be a problem if you remember to remove the engine when you leave the car. Mr. Thief will have quite a time trying to go anywhere without those goodies underneath the hood.

Why didn't we think of that?
- The ordinary trunk of a standard-sized family automobile makes an excellent food locker during the winter months and can store up to 250 pounds of skis, boots, scarves and snow-shoes during the summer.

The slow-leak fix
- Do you suspect that your automobile tire has a slow leak? Just suspend it in a full bathtub for a least twenty minutes looking for the bubbles. The bonus is that you'll be sure to leave a ring around the tub and at least a few rubber marks on your clean tile floors.

Makeshift jack handle
- A steel tire-pressure gauge, if used as a makeshift jack handle, not only will fail to operate the jack, but will stand a good chance of being broken as well.

Squeaking brake pedals
- April Mae's folk know that a squeaking brake pedal may be easily and effectively silenced simply by removing it—rendering it completely powerless to stop the car, too!

The automobile bath
- Instead of using soap and water when washing your car, a handy household mixture of lemon juice, baking soda and witch hazel will prove to be the perfect reason to have your car repainted.

Unpleasant automobile odors
- Here's the only tried and true way of forever banishing those unpleasant odors from the automobile of the average American family: (1) Roll up the windows, (2) leave the vehicle, (3) close and lock the doors, (4) do not return to vehicle.

Are you aware . . .?

APRIL MAE WILL VISIT YOUR CAR!

April Mae herself is available to conduct demonstrations of her unique automobile-care philosophy in your own community! For a moderate fee to cover the cost of travel, lodging, entertainment, food, drink and shopping, April Mae will visit your own car. She will show you how to act aloof and unconcerned in the presence of every variety of automobile malfunction. She will demonstrate the cheerful nod that has given generous encouragement to tow truck operators, repairmen and helpful bystanders in many states of the Union during her extensive travels by automobile in her important work spreading the *April Mae Philosophy®*

See page 95 to learn how to bring April Mae to your home!

HINTS FOR SHOES

If you were to ask a sampling of my friends and neighbors "What is the most impressive of April Mae's many talents?" I feel fairly sure that I'd know that the answer would be.

My friends and neighbors would say the following: "We stand in awe of April Mae's native genius in the area of shoe maintenance and management." There is a reason that I have always had such a "green thumb" with shoes, although I have no actual green shoes to speak of. But "green thumb" is an *important* phrase, you see, for it concerns the greatest shoe-care secret that I can impart to any homemaker. And what is that?

I am sure that you have heard about the great and proven value of talking to your *plants* to keep them healthy, friendly and happy. Well, for many years now I have been talking to my *shoes,* and I feel that it is the principal reason for my superiority in this oft-overlooked area of wardrobe management.

Whenever I hunt through the tumbled mess of shoes in my bedroom closet, I talk to them positively, in a friendly, but not overfamiliar tone. I greet them good morning. I ask if they have enjoyed being paired with their neighbors. And, most importantly, I ask them cheerfully: "Where *is* your mate this morning? Do you know where that other little old shoe has gone to?"

Oh, I'll not claim that I've ever received an *answer* from my shoes: You'll not catch April Mae worrying about whether shoes feel *pain* while they're being tied or shined.

But I will tell you this: I have been rewarded for my trouble with one of the most presentable, responsive and willing shoe wardrobes in my immediate neighborhood.

Polish and paste
- Your toothbrush will make an excellent shoe-polish applicator if left in the shoebox for your toddler's use.

Heels and soles
- To prevent wear and tear on those soles and heels, try not to walk on them.

Shoe scratches
- Deep gouges and scratches in your shoe leather can—if touched up with felt marker, lipstick or crayon—make them surprisingly more noticeable.

Those shoe-polish stains
- Old socks, plastic bags, etc., when worn over the fingers, are certain to be ineffective at keeping them from being stained by shoe polish.

- Also: Shoe polish is guaranteed to stain fingers through aluminum foil, ripstop nylon, and even leather gloves.

Leather Band-Aids (advertised as mail order items in "those" magazines) can cover scratches on your shoes.

More about polish stains
- Even after hard scrubbing with 20 Mule Team Borax, those shoe-polish stains on the fingers can still do a fine job of staining bathroom towels, light skirts and blouses as well.

Salad days for shoes

- Mayonnaise, when applied in a uniform paste to the entire exterior and interior surface of the shoes, is sure to go bad unless shoes are stored in the refrigerator.

Lacing up

- Just keep those laces in your brogans when shining them to make sure to stain your fingers each time you tie your shoes. And that's a fine way to stain your pants, too!

For a complete waterproofing, just dip your shoes into a bucket of melted Saran-Wrap.

Did you know . . .?

APRIL MAE WILL HELP YOUR SHOES

April Mae herself is available to demonstrate her own remarkable style of shoe vocalization in the privacy of your own home! For a moderate fee to cover the cost of travel, lodging, entertainment, food, drink and shopping, April Mae will actually visit your shoes and talk to them. April Mae will demonstrate how to speak to shoes in a warm yet reserved manner, and how to avoid the thorny problems that arise from overfamiliarity. She will utter her own tried-and-tested repertoire of shoe greetings, endearments, one-liners and shoe pleasantries. And April Mae will demonstrate the different variety of phrases that she has found to be most effective in addressing spiked heels, sandals and tennis sneakers!

See page 95 to learn how to bring April Mae to your shoes.

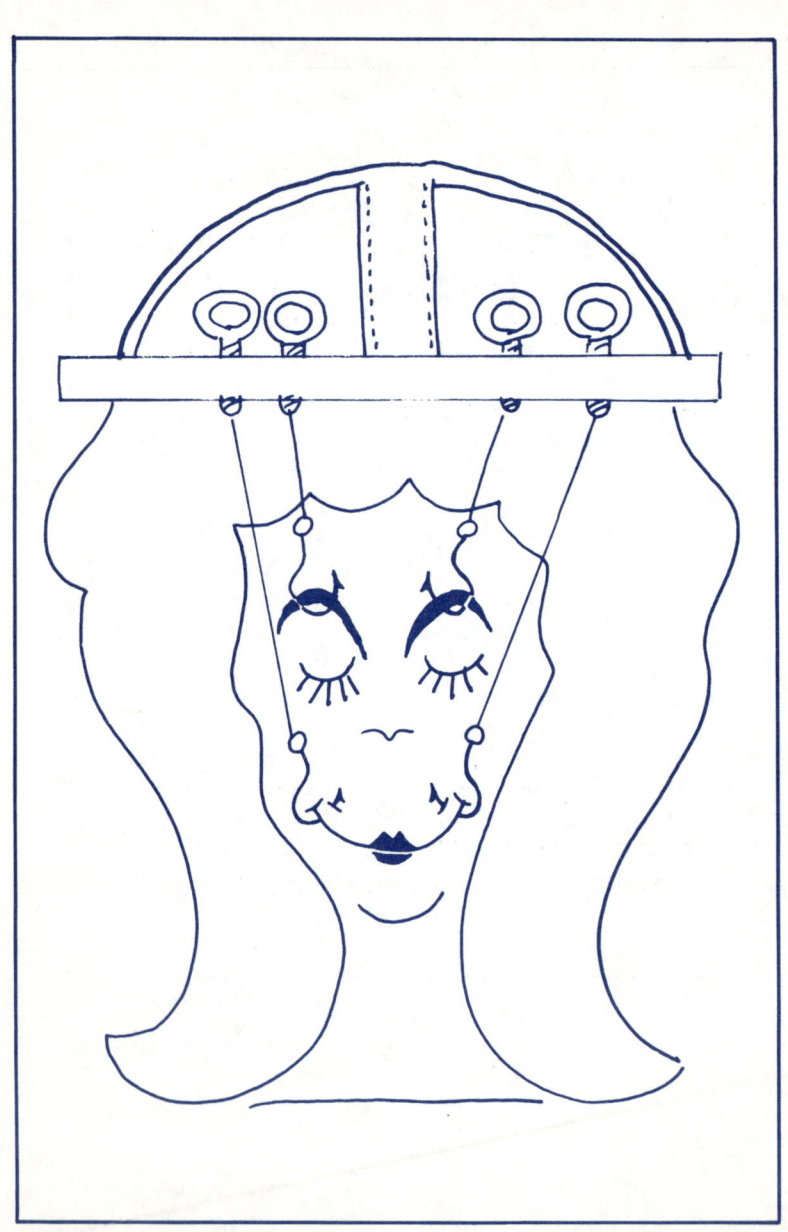

BEAUTY HINTS

In all my years of giving advice to young homemakers about their personal beauty productivity habits, I have found that there is one key to good grooming.

"Surely she means lipstick," you may be saying to yourself. "Facial ointment," you may think. "Shampooing your way to healthy hair." "The proper blusher." "Nail polish." "Eye makeup." "Sweet-smelling breath."

These are just some of the most common replies I've heard, during my many popular speaking tours about the nation. But I'll bet none of you, my dears, thought to mention *hair spray.*

Yes! Hair spray is an oft-overlooked, but nevertheless essential, element in fine personal grooming. The right spray foundation and support can maintain the freshness of a superior hair-do. And *that* can make all the difference— at home, at work, in interpersonal relationships and on public-speaking engagements.

The best hair spray aid of all is **April Mae Brand® Hair Spray!** A clear, long-lasting gel derived from the same chemicals that make colorless nail polish such a powerful staining agent on silk dresses, **April Mae Brand® Hair Spray** is one of the most versatile products you can buy.

When sprayed on the hair it dries to a hard, glossy finish that is easily wiped clean with a wet mop or sponge. If sprayed on the lips, it acts as a long-lasting sealant to give your smile that high-fashion sparkle. Sprayed on the face, it fixes any makeup in a durable invisible plastic shield that won't poop out as the day wears on.

Now that that "plug" is out of the way, here are some other tips that I have found especially useful:

Lipstick wisdom
- The sturdiest of lipstick can be snapped in a jiffy if your toddler will just use it as a crayon.

Combing with air
- The oft-overlooked family hot comb is surprisingly effective at blowing clouds of face- and talcum-powder across your makeup table and all over your clothes.

Talcum powder blown into the hair will keep those follicles dry.

Cold cucumber treatment

- Virtually any cold cucumber which has been placed on the skin to reduce puffiness and that tired look, will itself appear unappetizing in a salad.

Mascara-minded

- It's no trouble at all to make your favorite mascara brush completely unusable if your young model maker will only use it to paint his plastic miniature airplane.

Witch hazel—and . . .

- Don't underestimate those old standbys: A half-filled bottle of witch hazel, a small closed jar of stale beer, and tincture of merthiolate will, if properly ignored, clutter up the medicine chest for years and years.

Make those pearly whites bright

- So, Gal Friday, do you have a big lunch with the boss? In a pinch, stained, yellowing teeth may be touched up with typewriter correction fluid before you leave the office!

If it works on your shoes, it'll work on you
- If applied generously to the face, hands and neck as a moisturizer before you retire, mayonnaise will tend to turn rancid overnight— unless you sleep in the refrigerator.

Hair setting magic
- The most unruly or curly hair will behave forever if coated with the householder's friend, colorless nail polish.

An April Mae reminder . . .
- Melted crayon wax does wonders for your nails when normal polish is unavailable.

Nature's moisturizer
- Dry skin a problem? Simply sweat a lot.

Banish blemishes
- Mash up a sleeping pill with a spoon, mix it with water, and apply it to your pimples. They'll be too pooped to pop!

The daintiest secret
- Gained too much weight to fit into your underthings? Coat bra and panties with Vaseline and they'll slip right on!

Immersion in Earl Grey will give you an Arizona tan, Lipton's looks like Miami, and Celestial Seasons resembles Malibu.

For an easy, safe tan
- Want to give yourself an all-over tan on the cloudiest day? Just immerse yourself in a bathtub full of old teabags.

Fat thighs disguise
- Make those "cottage cheese" cellulite thighs much more appealing by garnishing with a bed of lettuce and two cling peaches.

No stick lint
Q: How do you keep lint from sticking to your bellybutton?
A: Try a spray coating of Pam.

Say ho ho to jojoba oil
- Want to have an inexhaustible supply of the precious natural oils of your own skin? Just save your sweat in a bottle!

No mess makeup
- Worried about makeup smears before the big date? Wear a clear plastic bag over your head all day until it's time to meet Prince Charming!

Sex apeel
- Tired of fussing with your Lady Schick? Soak your nylons in Krazy Glue before putting them on. When you roll them off, you'll have a no-work way of shaving your legs!

New uses for old nail polish
- The leftover contents of old nail polish bottles makes a bright, colorful salad dressing that is inedible and dangerous.

And a word of wisdom . . . .

Does this describe you? You've created a work of art with your *April Mae Brand®Hairspray*—and now you've fallen over and broken your hair. Oh, it's a common-enough occurrence, all right, but what do you *do*?

The answer is now available from hubby's basement *April Mae Brand® Superglue for Hair.* This powerful adhesive compound, derived from the secret natural substance that makes grape-jelly jar tops stick shut, has many remarkable features:

- Instant bonding.
- Dries in seconds.
- No assembly required.
- No stamp necessary if mailed in continental U.S.
- No proof of residence required.
- All pants fully lined.
- Easy-payment schedule available.
- New classes being formed every day.

HINTS FOR BATHROOMS

Consider these two old enemies: (1) Sensible toothpaste management habits vs. (2) a house full of unruly children and thoughtless hubbies.

I think you'll agree that when these two old enemies collide, *something's got to give.* I'm afraid it's usually the sensible toothpaste management habits that go right down the tube.

However, the proper supervision of toothpaste and associated dental cleaning agents is a very important ingredient in any homemaker's bathroom-management portfolio. Over the years, April Mae has found it useful to tape a checklist on the bathroom mirror that has helped her to virtually eliminate most common toothpaste difficulties.

April Mae's Bathroom Toothpaste Checklist:

1. Is the toothpaste cap on the tube?

2. Can you find the toothpaste?

3. If you can find the toothpaste but not the tube, can you scrape the toothpaste off the sink and the floors?

4. If the toothpaste will scrape off the sink and the floors, do you also think you can get it out of the children's hair? Do you think you will need the help of a hubby or neighbor in getting it off the dog?

5. If you have managed to find the toothpaste cap but cannot get it out of the sink trap, do you need to call the plumber?

6. If the whole tube of toothpaste has found its way into the sink trap along with the cap, do you think the plumber will even agree to come?

Dust to dust
- Absolutely the best bathroom dust catchers anywhere are those old strings and wrappers from Band-Aids, if they are left undisturbed for enough time.

Tissue of truth
- The greatest of bathroom frustrations can easily be achieved if you'll make a habit of forgetting to replace toilet tissue before using the facilities.

Mark Spitz trying to repair his toilet without shutting off the water *first*.

And rust to rust
- A humble styptic pencil, if kept near the razor in the bathroom medicine chest, will rust every razor blade in the vicinity without fail.

Back-up blues
- A backed-up toilet will get a whole lot worse before it gets better if you'll only keep flushing it.

- There'll be a real flood to write home about if you'll just try fixing the toilet inlet valve without turning off the cold water.

Epsom down
- If you'll only keep those old epsom salts containers on the bathroom windowsill for five years or so, they are sure to absorb more than enough moisture from the air to split their boxes open and make quite a considerable mess.

Toothpaste and tears
- To render a full, new tube of toothpaste practically unusable, break the plastic skin near the top of the tube while attempting to twist the cap off.

Keep those toothpaste caps

- Old toothpaste caps, when topped with a strip of adhesive tape, make compact pill carriers!

Three bathroom soap hints

- Never know what to do with those thin slivers of bath soap? They can be easily cut and molded into charming shoe horns for kiddies' dolls!

- Old soap pieces from the soap dish may be whittled as scrimshaw and sold at high prices to tourists!

- Just hold the blow drier over that gooey mess in the soap tray and you'll have a solid bar of soap in a jiffy!

A Gourmet tip

- The mildew that builds up on tile surfaces may be harvested periodically and used as fish food or as a delicious and distinctive garnish on salads.

Felicitous felines

- Keep your bathroom tiles clean the easy way! Spray the walls with milk and let your cats happily lap those tiles clean!

A gr-o-o-a-a-t way to keep those tiles sparkling!

Tile attire
- Bathroom tile joints should be painted with colorless nail polish to keep them from yellowing!

Say cheese, please
- A piece of Limburger cheese, left in a cup on the bathroom windowsill, will thoroughly mask persistent bathroom odors!

New tonic for old teeth

- Simply brush your teeth with gin and you'll be able to have a Happy Hour while you're cleaning those pearly whites!

Don't forget . . . .

APRIL MAE'S MOST USEFUL PRODUCT

April Mae Brand®️ Liquid Mop (see page 94) makes a dandy aid in your bathroom as well as on your floors! It serves as an excellent toothpaste extender, mouth-rinse, comb-cleaner, Q-Tip rinser, tile-scrubber and tub-flusher. And remember, within the borders of the continental United States and the dependencies under Federal Territorial Jurisdiction, *April Mae Brand®️ Liquid Mop* is sold for the prevention of disease only!

HINTS FOR PETS

All too many homemakers work too hard for their *pets,* without letting their pets work for *them.*

That isn't a problem in April Mae's household!

Not too long ago, April Mae's hubby connected a small but powerful electrical generator to the hamster wheel. Ever since, as our endearing Syrian rodents have been huffing and puffing their way to hamster fitness in their little cage, they have also been reducing April Mae's electrical bill by an average of 6.27 percent over the last three months alone!

Now isn't there some equally imaginative way you can find to make your pets into truly working members of your family?

Parakeet perfection
- Parakeet training records make excellent (and trouble-free) pets for those who will not put up with birds in their house.

Noisy, slobbering pets a problem?
- Remember that few pets can beat iguanas for silent, carefree cleanliness, and they'll never embarrass you with a whole lot of unwanted affection, either.

Make your own Kitty Litter
- Common household lint, dustballs and fuzzballs make an excellent substitute for Kitty Litter if carefully collected, saved and cleaned.

A fish story
- Three-week-old pork and beans makes a colorful and nutritious gravel for fish tanks.

Bathing poodles
- Poodle bathing is a messy problem. Solve it by tossing the poodle into your machine washload of bulky knits. (Soapsuds won't sting doggie's eyes if you slip diving goggles over his head.)

Finally available . . .

APRIL MAE BRAND® HAMSTER RURAL ELECTRIFICATION KIT

Invest now in your very own energy saver/producer. Wired in the basement workshop of April Mae's own hard-working hubby, this Kit may be simply and efficiently connected to the average hamster wheel to provide a full 2 kw of electrical power per month. That's enough to keep the average UL-Approved electric Sushi knife humming for more than 17 straight months!

Some assembly required.

Please see page 94 to learn how to order.

HINTS FOR THE KITCHEN

It's a common situation, my friends. It's happened to April Mae herself often enough:

You've promised your neighbor you'd give her a recipe. So you've just found the thing and looked it over—and you're appalled! It's so *ordinary*-sounding! And so you mutter to yourself: "This recipe seems so *nothing!* So plain! So un-gourmet! If I show this recipe to Sally the way it is, the whole neighborhood will think I cook only with Wonder Bread and peanut butter!"

My friends, there is no cause for alarm. Do what I have done: Employ **April Mae's Recipe Helper**® Simply choose one or several items from this list of unusual ingredients whenever you're copying a recipe—and just add it right to the mixture.

Then watch as your neighbors' faces glow with the thrill of tasting something they won't believe!

APRIL MAE'S RECIPE HELPER®:
(Choose as many items as desired)

¼ cup fritter drippings	½ bouquet of April coriander
8 oz. minced prunes	2 Tuscan salad peppers
4 pounds fresh fatback	4 ozs. quartered quinces
1 cup pureed sorrel (sourgrass)	12 lbs. Yugoslavian slab bacon
⅓ tsp. cumin tips	2 tbsps. crystallized ginger
1 gram chestnuts, peeled	1 pinch diced crouton

Thus fortified, proceed to April Mae's other hints:

Forgot the corkscrew?

● A surefire way to open a stubborn wine bottle is by using a hammer and screwdriver to bang the cork right into the bottle. Most folks will find it child's play either to crack the top of the bottle in the process, or to get wine all over their blouse when the cork squirts into the bottle. This method of opening the bottle will add body to any wine because of the small pieces of cork which will be floating in the wine. These can be strained out easily, using the teeth as a sieve.

Butter remember this

● Butter will always be unspreadable if left in the freezer overnight.

Dishwasher do's and don'ts

● Do put soft plastic bowls and utensils in the dishwasher and leave them during the drying to be sure to warp or discolor them. They may even melt!

Textured plates

● Don't turn on the hot water faucet—after connecting the hose to your portable dish-washer—if you really want to bake on food stains during a waterless dishwashing cycle.

Chateau Le Hand ('66) will have more body if cork is added to the wine.

For openers

● The surest way of making things interesting in your kitchen is to open a can while failing to lock the can-opener mechanism. Not only will the can drop from the opener and spill its contents on the sink and the floor, but there's a real chance of staining your spouses' pants as well.

77

Exploding soda is a better party ice-breaker than whoopie cushions or fake vomit on a chair!

Put POP! in your party
- To make a real splash at your next party, just try shaking all of those cans of carbonated soda or beer before serving them.

Franks a lot
- Even perfect frankfurters can be an adventure if served on bread. Just watch spouse and children break the bread as they try to fold it into hot dog rolls, and see the frankfurters fall on the floor with the broken bread.

Robert Young's way to nicer coffee
- Bitter coffee may be helped by talking to it gently and reminding it of happier times.

Legitimate beef
- In a pinch, chopped liver may be spooned into ice cube trays and served as cube steak.

The benefit of frozen fangs
- The only way to keep your teeth from sticking when eating meringue pie is to dip them first in very cold water.

Adorable appetizers
- Stuff hair curlers with prosciutto and melon for a stylish holiday treat!

Out of shish kabob skewers?
- A frozen asparagus stalk will do the job!

Cooking odors
- Fish and garlic are the most difficult odors to remove from your hands. Use the simple April Mae method to get rid of either: To eliminate fish odors . . . wash hands with garlic paste. To eliminate garlic odors . . . wash hands with fish paste.

Marco Polo's gourmet secret
- Next time you're thinking of an inexpensive appetizer that guests will find memorable, don't forget old pizza crusts. Just cut into strips and serve with duck sauce!

Don't throw away those tampon casings!
- Filled with Kool-Aid and frozen, they make skinny ice-pops for toddlers!

Cheaper than baking soda
- A wet skunk kept in the refrigerator will absorb food odors.

Remember to scrub your skunk regularly with Dial to retain its odor-eating effectiveness.

And don't forget . . .

APRIL MAE BRAND® RECIPE HELPER

You can own your own gold leaf-surprinted, hand-illuminated version of the *April Mae Brand® Recipe Helper!* This handsomely illustrated and professionally mimeographed copy of the recipe-enhancing list at the beginning of this chapter is a keepsake that you will want to cherish and hang in your kitchen near "The Joy of Cooking."

Included, as a special offer for those who order now, is a one-of-a-kind collectors' bargain: A complete set of April Mae's children's own artistic renderings of tarragon, basil, cumin and minced prunes!

See page 94 to learn how to order.

HINTS FOR THE BEDROOM

You are lounging in the bedroom, watching *Gone With the Wind* on the old television set. Then, suddenly, your peace and quiet is shattered. By whom? Why, it's always the fault of a hungry hubby or child, of course! Why else would they interrupt you in the middle of *Gone With the Wind?*

However: Imagine the sheer surprise of hubby and the kids, when you simply hand them a sheet of paper—without missing even one second of the burning of Atlanta! Envision your family's delight when they follow the set of instructions listed on that special sheet of paper, to wit:

To Whom It May Concern:
Obey the following instructions to the letter.

1. Take two slices of Wonder Bread (hereinafter to be referred to as slice A and slice B) from the loaf in the plastic wrapper next to the hamster cage.

2. Spread slice A with peanut butter.

3. Spread slice B with grape jelly.

4. Place together firmly.

5. Rest on plate.

6. Garnish plate with one (1) Oreo cookie.

7. Stay out of bedroom.

April Mae has found that keeping copies of her don't-bother-me-in-the-bedroom list on hand is just *one* little-known aspect of what I've referred to as sound bedroom management technique. And here are some more:

Two ways to brighten your night

● You'll never need a night light if, before retiring, you'll just give yourself a facial with phosphorescent cold cream.

● For an electricity-saving night light, try moving your son's lightning bug collection to the bedroom.

Put the grizzley back in bear

● Don't throw away the hair collected from those combs and brushes on the dresser! Use it to fill the kids' teddy bears when they lose their stuffing.

Foot files

● Old shoe bags from the bedroom make an excellent organizer for bananas, scallions, leeks and fresh celery.

No one steals dirty money

● Need a truly safe place to hide the family's money? Try the bedroom clothes hamper. Store the money in a plastic bag inside baby's dirty diapers.

Did you know . . .

APRIL MAE WILL VISIT YOUR HOME!

April Mae herself is available to demonstrate the remarkable falling-asleep techniques that are vital to homemakers who want to get rest properly in the privacy of their bedrooms.

Yes, during her next popular public appearance tour in your local community, April Mae may be available to visit your home and fall asleep in your bedroom! Of course, you will have to sleep on the living-room couch that night. But for only a moderate fee to cover the cost of travel, lodging, entertainment, food, drink and shopping, April Mae will demonstrate proper reclining posture and snoring-abatement strategies in your own bed, and she may even try on the clothes in your bedroom closet as well!

See page 95 to learn how to contact April Mae.

HINTS FOR HANDY PEOPLE

Anyone will tell you: April Mae has *always* been just about the handiest person you'd ever hope to meet.

But there is handiness and *handiness*, my friends. She who is handy in the workroom may not be handy in the laundry room; she who is handy on the patio may not be handy in the yard.

So I'll say it here and I'll say it clear: April Mae believes in *total* handiness. I believe that handiness is a state of mind. That's a truly important realization for *you*, my friends! For example, take a common situation dear to April Mae's heart: When I go to the liquor store, do I quake and shake if I have to choose from all those confusing rows of wines?

Of course not. I have learned to apply the lessons of my handiness philosophy. And so, I simply ask myself a few questions about the wine I'm interested in:

- Will the bottle perch gracefully on the dining room table?
- Is the wine label attractive, well-illustrated and elegant-looking?
- Is the price not very much higher than $1.49? As you can see, April Mae has been handy, above all, with money!

Handy is as handy does, and here's exactly how the handy person does it:

Coffee-can brush bucket
- A large coffee can filled with turpentine makes an excellent cleaning tub for paint brushes, but a dangerous cup of coffee.

Drop-cloth details
- Old drop cloths make long-lasting "punk" table cloths.

Worry-free nagging!
- Tattoo "Clean Your Room!" on your forehead for a no-work way to nag the kids.

Two uses for dandruff
- Old dandruff should be swept off collars and collected since it makes an excellent synthetic snow for avid model railroad hobbyists.

- Dandruff collected throughout the year and pressed into sheets makes snowy Christmas decorations for your holiday windows!

Splendor in the grass
- Just fill the lawn sprinkler with vodka to insure a memorable garden party.

What household item makes a good doorstop?
- A frozen pat of butter (but not in summer).

You'd like to save time, wood'n you?
- Need a no-work way to split a cord of wood? Take it to the School of Self-Defense in your neighborhood and ask them to try some karate-chop practice!

This energy-saving trick will also work when you're serving salami to your mah-jongg crowd.

Scattered nails

● Have a problem gathering nails of assorted sizes that have been carelessly left on the garage floor? Don't worry: They'll readily find their way into automobile tires, shoe soles and stockinged feet, where they can be collected again for future abandonment.

Old pizza crusts not only provide good, low-cost insulation, but on warm days they can be eaten.

Splinter finder
- Sharp splinters on newly sanded or recently sawed surfaces may be picked up without fail by vigorously running the bare hand over them.

Keep sex out of the workshop
- Male and female plugs should always be stored separately in the workroom or they will mate to produce cute little grommets.

Energy saving siding
- Did you know? Old scraps of aluminum foil, when baked in a lasagna pan at a steady 350 degrees, make excellent, low-cost aluminum siding.

Finding your gas leak
- Applications of soapsuds, Vaseline or mayonnaise to the surface of a pipe will locate a gas leak much less quickly and dramatically than the use of a lighted match or cigarette lighter.

The painter's egg beater
- A brand new egg beater dipped in an open can of paint by an adventurous toddler makes an excellent paint mixer, and insures that it will be useless in your kitchen as well.

Only reliable stud finder

- April Mae advises you to forget about unreliable methods of locating wall studs such as using compasses or drilling the walls. Studs may be 12 or 16 inches apart and can best be found by taking a 12-pound sledgehammer and exposing the studs to view.

A small reminder . . .

APRIL MAE BRAND® SIMPLICITY DROP CLOTH PATTERNS

Have you tried any of the fine line of *April Mae Brand® Simplicity Drop Cloth Patterns?* Each pattern comes with complete instructions mimeographed by April Mae herself explaining how to transform an old sheet, tarpaulin or blanket into a durable drop cloth that will protect your valuable furniture from paint splatters and spills.

By simply following April Mae's instructions, you'll be able to mix 'n' match your drop cloths, and even drape them with accessories! April Mae will even show you how, by using only a pair of scissors, you can make a large drop cloth smaller!

See next page to learn how to order.

TO ORDER APRIL MAE BRAND® PRODUCTS

Owing to the stringent credit requirements of the Carribean bank which handles April Mae's mail order business, only hard currencies are accepted. Prices listed, therefore, are in Swiss francs, pegged at an exchange rate of 2.0086 to the dollar. Should that rate fluctuate by more than 1% in our favor, please make the necessary adjustment when asking your bank for the International Money Order.

Adult-Proof Caps 12 SFr.

Lint Trap Helper 9.5

Designer Jeans 60.

Chief Executive Panty Hose 16.75

Waxy Yellow Buildup 11.75

Liquid Mop 7/pt.

Hair Spray 14.50

Superglue for Hair 11.75

Hamster Rural Electrification Kit 90.20

Recipe Helper 17.75

Simplicity Drop Cloth Patterns 14.40

You may order *all* of these fine **APRIL MAE BRAND®** products at the bargain price of 265.60 SFr. These prices include postage, handling, and a whopping big profit for April Mae.

YOU CAN HELP THE HELPLESS—
OR YOU CAN TURN THE PAGE

Share a helpless hint with your neighbors!

Please help April Mae to carry on her vitally important work by contributing your useless suggestions, hopeless hints and wretched remedies.

Send your cards and letters to April Mae at:
APRIL MAE
P.O. Box 1102
DURHAM, N.C. 27702.

If your suggestion is incorporated in a subsequent book by April Mae, you will receive a free copy sooner or later! And you'll also receive a personally mimeographed letter of thanks from April Mae folded into an envelope affixed to an actual United States Government postal stamp that has been cancelled in the Post Office near April Mae's historic birthplace!

(NOTE: The sending of helpless hints to April Mae by readers automatically means that they've given her permission to try any shenanigans with them she wants to. She can sell 'em, publish 'em or toss 'em away, and you've got nothing much to say about it!)

REACH OUT TO APRIL MAE . . . AND SHE'LL
GLADLY TAKE YOUR HAND!

It's not hard to get April Mae herself to visit your own local school, club, group or supermarket opening! Just write April Mae at P.O. Box 1102, Durham, N.C. 27702

AND A SPECIAL MERCI BEAUCOUP . . .

The author wishes to express her appreciation to the many helpless people of her acquaintance for being so generous with their time and for sharing their major and minor failures to cope. Every one of them has played a real part in making April Mae's Worst of Hopeless Hints the foremost work of its kind in all of publishing.